Theophilus Haddock, Edward Tatham

Error Detected and Fiction Rebuked

In a Letter to Edward Tatham

Theophilus Haddock, Edward Tatham

Error Detected and Fiction Rebuked
In a Letter to Edward Tatham

ISBN/EAN: 9783337292911

Printed in Europe, USA, Canada, Australia, Japan

Cover: Foto ©Thomas Meinert / pixelio.de

More available books at **www.hansebooks.com**

AND

FICTION REBUKED:

In a LETTER to

EDWARD TATHAM, D. D. so called,

and Rector of Lincoln-College, Oxford.

ON HIS

SERMON, 1st Epistle John iv. 1.

Which (for its Excellence) was read in four
Parish Worship-Houses, in the Year 1792, and
published under the Title of " A Sermon
" suitable to the Times. "

By THEOPHILUS HADDOCK.

LONDON:

PRINTED FOR THE AUTHOR:

And Sold by the Booksellers in Town and Country.

M DCC XCIV.

[Price SIXPENCE.]

ERROR DETECTED, &c.

EDWARD TATHAM,

THY fermon on " Try the fpirits, &c."
came not to my hand till lately, and then
I perufed it hoping that as thou filleft fo high
a ftation as an inftructor of others for the priefthood, it would have furnifhed me with fome
edifying knowledge, as the text contains fuch
excellent advice; but being difappointed in my
expectation, I thought it neither an uncivil or
unkind employ, to communicate fome things
that have occurred to my mind upon reading
it. I fee the drift is to juftify Epifcopacy, and
to render other minifters as intruders and inva-
lid, which appears to me to be by no means
proved; but as thou acknowledgeft the fcriptures to be the fource from whence thy authority for fuch doctrine is derived, I truft I fhall
be able, from that holy book, to prove thou
art very much in error in thy judgment and
conclufions; for the very early part of it in-
ftructs

ftructs us, that there were worfhippers when there was no prieft: and I believe there will be again, and that acceptable, as well as unacceptable: nor do I believe they were felf-taught, nor was their father before them, but had an higher inftructor than the moft dignified collegian that ever the world produced.

I am glad thou haft chofe the facred fcriptures for thy authorities for endeavouring to eftablifh thy principles, becaufe I fhall take the fame to prove how very much thou erreft in thy difcourfe, from their facred information, inftruction, and doctrine: for they tell us that God by his fpirit inftructed common artificers in their trade, even to work in blue, fcarlet, &c. It was God that inftructed Noah that the earth was corrupt, and that all flefh had corrupted their ways before him; but, for all this, his fagacity could not have devifed and conftructed the ark, for the prefervation of himfelf and family, had not Divine Wifdom inftructed him. Abraham, I believe, would not have thought that the life of his fon would have been an acceptable offering, had not the communication been immediately from the Divine Source. Mofes would have known nothing of the time or manner of the redemption of the children of Ifrael out of Egypt, nor that he was to be the inftrument to effect it, had not Divine Communication been the channel by which he received it; nor could he by any other means have

have come to the knowledge that a tabernacle was to be built, how conftructed, the wor-fhip in it performed, or which tribe it was the divine purpofe to elect to be priefts and minifters of it. And thou mayeft remember, that though they were of and by the immediate appointment of the Moft High, two of them loft their lives by their prefumption, in offering ftrange fire before the Lord: and I have often thought this ought to be a leffon of awful in-ftruction to all that fpeak in his name, whether in the eftablifhment, or under any other deno-mination; for as no man knoweth the things of a man, fave the fpirit of a man that is in him—fo no man knoweth the things of God, but by the fpirit of God.—Pleafe to read the fecond chapter of Paul's firft Epiftle to the Corinthians. How prefumptuous, therefore, muft it be for any to fpeak in His name, with any authority or qualification lefs than this!

But to proceed: All the wifdom and policy of men could never have devifed the Urim and Thummim; and much lefs have given it the power of communicating light and knowledge with refpect to outward events and occurrences: then how much inferior muft they be for giving light and knowledge of divine things, but as themfelves are immediately inftructed from the fource of all knowledge both natural and divine. Had Mofes compounded the holy anointing oil for the prieft's office, without divine direction.

conceivelt thou that it would have been an acceptable fervice in him? I conclude that neither thou, nor any other rational man, can believe any fuch thing; and yet how many men are there that take upon them the very office of the priefthood, by a practice which I am perfuaded is much more prefumptuous than it would have been in him only to have made the oil—though I am of the judgment that if he had, the query propofed to fome under his difpenfation, would with holy indignation have been addreffed to him, " Who hath required this at thy hand?"

We may obferve, that though Divine Mercy had minutely given direction about the tabernacle, and all it's fervices, the priefts foon corrupted the ordinances of God and chofe their own ways. Eli, the high-prieft, becaufe he did not reftrain his fons and punifh their villainy, and other his practices in the mal-adminiftration of the law, died of a broken neck; and his two fons, who were both priefts, for their wickednefs in that they oppreffed the people and violated the ordinances of the Moft High, loft their lives in battle. Now I would have all priefts and minifters of every denomination take folemn warning by thefe, and remember that though they could boaft a divinely legal ordination, that was no protection to fecure them from the hand of Divine Juftice for difhonouring him before the people: and if that ordination and qualification, which was of his own appointment

have come to the knowledge that a tabernacle was to be built, how conftructed, the worfhip in it performed, or which tribe it was the divine purpofe to elect to be priefts and minifters of it. And thou mayeft remember, that though they were of and by the immediate appointment of the Moft High, two of them loft their lives by their prefumption, in offering ftrange fire before the Lord: and I have often thought this ought to be a leffon of awful inftruction to all that fpeak in his name, whether in the eftablifhment, or under any other denomination; for as no man knoweth the things of a man, fave the fpirit of a man that is in him— fo no man knoweth the things of God, but by the fpirit of God.—Pleafe to read the fecond chapter of Paul's firft Epiftle to the Corinthians. How prefumptuous, therefore, muft it be for any to fpeak in His name, with any authority or qualification lefs than this !

But to proceed: All the wifdom and policy of men could never have devifed the Urim and Thummim; and much lefs have given it the power of communicating light and knowledge with refpect to outward events and occurrences: then how much inferior muft they be for giving light and knowledge of divine things, but as themfelves are immediately inftructed from the fource of all knowledge both natural and divine. Had Mofes compounded the holy anointing oil for the prieft's office, without divine direction.

conceiveft

conceivest thou that it would have been an acceptable service in him? I conclude that neither thou, nor any other rational man, can believe any such thing; and yet how many men are there that take upon them the very office of the priesthood, by a practice which I am persuaded is much more presumptuous than it would have been in him only to have made the oil—though I am of the judgment that if he had, the query proposed to some under his dispensation, would with holy indignation have been addressed to him, " Who hath required this at thy hand ?"

We may observe, that though Divine Mercy had minutely given direction about the tabernacle, and all it's services, the priests soon corrupted the ordinances of God and chose their own ways. Eli, the high-priest, because he did not restrain his sons and punish their villainy, and other his practices in the mal-administration of the law, died of a broken neck; and his two sons, who were both priests, for their wickedness in that they oppressed the people and violated the ordinances of the Most High, lost their lives in battle. Now I would have all priests and ministers of every denomination take solemn warning by these, and remember that though they could boast a divinely legal ordination, that was no protection to secure them from the hand of Divine Justice for dishonouring him before the people: and if that ordination and qualification, which was of his own appointment

ment, was no protection to them in their iniqui-
ty, I would have others that have but a spurious
one of men's devising, awfully consider that he
is a jealous God, and will not give his glory to
another, or his praise to graven images or the
religious devices of men's invention.

I think the first political priest that we read of,
who was of a king's making, was Amaziah,
priest of Bethel, or Jeroboam's chapel, or calf-
house; and this stimulated him with such conse-
quence as to forbid the Lord's prophet to declare
his message, his priestly authority qualifying him
so to act, as the other was but a poor shepherd
and a gatherer of sycamore fruit. I have
thought that political establishments, in all
countries, have derived their authority from no
higher source than Amaziah did his, 1 Kings xii.
25—33. which was from Jeroboam, an usurper;
for the kings of the Lord's appointment that
were before him left the business of the tabernacle and priests to the immediate direction of Him
who to the present time remains the alone head
of the church, declaring Himself under a figure
to be the Vine, and his church the branches;
and that as the branch could not bear fruit of it-
self except it abode in the vine, neither could
his church except it abode in Him, John xv.
4, 5, 6, 7. When thou hast by experience learnt
the efficacy of this doctrine in thy own heart, I
know thy teaching, if thou art called to teach
at all, will be very different from what thy
" Sermon

" Sermon fuitable to the Times" holds out; and therefore I fhall juft take the liberty to animadvert on fome paffages in it, I hope with chriftian charity and invariable truth, as that is the ftandard we fhould all walk by in love; for without it we cannot poffibly be Chrift's difciples.

And now firft give me leave to fay, thy quotation and doctrine contradict each other. In page 1, thou quoteft Paul's exhortation to prove all things, and hold faft that which is good; and yet in pages 8 and 9, thou art fo far from allowing that liberty, that thou art preffing all into a perfuafion that men inftructed in the fciences at univerfities, are the only perfons that can point out the way of falvation clearly to them. Thou indeed admitteft that thofe that hear them have a right to judge of their doctrine, but perhaps waft not well aware of what follows from this admiffion, which is this, it fuppofeth that there is a principle of religious knowledge implanted in the human mind, that is capable of judging of truth and error; and this is a juft fuppofition, for fo there really is: and that the apoftle whofe words thou haft chofen for thy text well knew, and therefore inftructed the primitive, and all true chriftians, even to the end of the world, to attend to its teaching, and not to the antichrifts that then were, now are, or ever will be in the world; for he told them they had an unction from the Holy One, and knew all things; and that he had not written to them becaufe they
knew

knew not the truth, but becaufe they knew it, and that no lie was of it. And his brother Peter declared that no prophecy of the fcripture was of any private interpretation, and that holy men of God fpoke then as they were moved of the Holy Ghoft: and the anointing or unction of which John fpake, is given to all **men**, that they may know as much of them as concerns their falvation.

But thy query in page 4 fmells fo ftrong of that antichriftian fpirit, which was gone out from the apoftle's doctrine, that I think it needful to prefs it upon the minds of all that are in good earneft for their falvation, to practife that which thy text fo wifely recommends, and to try thy fpirit by thy doctrine, and let the holy fcriptures be the judge, and then I am perfuaded they will find thine to be of the very nature which John cautioned the Chriftian converts againft believing or receiving. The query hinted at above runs thus, " In matters of fuch " deep concern and difficult enquiry, how are " all men able to judge for themfelves?" Why I will tell thee how they are able, or may be enabled, and that is, not to mock God with vain words, Ephefians v. 6. but humbly to wait for that which the church, whereof thou art a member, hath prefcribed in a prayer in which fupplication is made for attaining of it; and that is the collect which fhe hath appointed to be read three days fucceffively, at the time that popery

hath

hath invented for her to call Whitfuntide, and runs in the following words, viz. "God who "at this time didst teach the hearts of thy faith- "ful people, by sending them the light of thy "Holy Spirit, grant us by the same spirit to "have a right judgment in all things, and ever- "more to rejoice in its holy comfort, through "the merits of Christ Jesus our Saviour, who "liveth and reigneth with thee, in the unity of "the same spirit, one God, world without end, "Amen." And so say I; for that rightly or- dained and dignified minister of the gospel of Christ, Paul, hath told us, and I believe that there is no rational mind that doth not experi- ence the truth of it; that a measure and mani- festation of the spirit is given to every man to profit withal, so that a minister made by the same power that Paul was, could never pro- pound a question of so Antichristian a nature, to raise such a doctrine from, that people must be dependent upon men for the knowledge of the way of salvation, that have studied and learnt the liberal arts, to explain what that way was, when Carpenters, Upholsterers, and Fish- ermen have declared it more clearly, perfectly, and emphatically, than any man instructed into it, after the wisdom of this world, ever did or could: "for not many wise, not many mighty, "not many noble, are called; for God hath "chosen the foolish things of this world to con- "found the wise, that no flesh may glory in his "presence." Therefore they that profess themfelves Chriſt's miniſters, ſhould never glory, nor lie againſt the truth as it is in him, and revealed in the ſcriptures with indubitable certainty, through faith that is in Chriſt Jeſus, as the gift of God, and not in the principles and doctrines of men, that are as to the true and genuine faith of Chriſt, reprobate; as all muſt be that teach that ſalvation is attainable in no other way than as the humanly ordained men may and do explain it. Oh! horrid deluſion! for the lip of truth hath declared that " this is life " eternal, to know the only true God, and " Jeſus Chriſt whom he hath ſent :" and that " no man knoweth the Father but the Son, and " he to whom the Son will reveal him;" ſo that this knowledge and attainment is by divine revelation, and not human information.

Having now practiſed thy advice, and tried thy ſpirit by the holy ſcriptures, and finding it to be oppoſite both to the apoſtle's and Chriſt's, I think thou canſt not ſuppoſe it the leaſt unjuſt concluſion, to ſay, that it clearly appears to be the very Antichriſt that the apoſtle cautioned the people of his time againſt, as that through the divine unction they knew all things, and that he did not write to inſtruct them in the knowledge of the truth, but to adviſe them to keep in the truth, and attend to it's holy inſtructions and monitions; that the antichriſts that were then in the world might not deceive them out of their ſouls, and money, as his gracious Lord had enjoined him

him and all his apoftles and minifters in the
work of the gofpel, as they had freely received
the gofpel from him, viz. the power of God to
minifter, fo they fhould freely, without money,
and without price, impart it to the people : and
here the prophet Ifaiah's allufion to the gofpel
difpenfation is clearly fulfilled, chap. lv. Pleafe
to read the whole of it; for my humble defire is
that Divine Wifdom may open thy eyes and
heart to fee how blind thou art to the fpirituality
of the gofpel of Chrift. And I am the more
concerned for thy illumination, as that to be
carnally minded is death, but to be fpiritually
minded is life and peace. Thy whole chain of
reafoning on the fubject of the neceffity of people's being taught by men in the things of God,
runs in full contradiction to the declaration of
the God of Truth; for he hath declared that the
people fhould all know him from the greateft to
the leaft, and they fhould not need fay every
man to his neighbour and brother, Know the
Lord : and this is a prophecy pointing to the
difpenfation of time in which God was not to be
worfhipped in ceremonies and carnal ordinances, but in fpirit and in truth.

Under the law the prieft's lips were to keep
knowledge, and the people were to feek the ex-
planation of the law from his mouth, as he was
indeed by divine appointment to be the Meffen-
ger of the Lord of Hofts; but all the legal
things in divine worfhip are done away in Chrift,

nor are there any acceptable worshippers of the Father in this day. but such that worship him in spirit and in truth; for such, said our blessed Saviour, the Father seeks to worship him. The wisdom of this world is declared to be foolishness with God; therefore I am persuaded that all the wisdom and knowledge that t. is world can furnish a man with, cannot make him a minister of the gospel, nor one whit more qualify him to judge of the truths of the gospel of Christ, nor in any degree so much as the most illiterate mechanic that hath been obedient to the teachings of the grace of God which bringeth salvation in and to his own heart. Please to read the five last verses of Paul's second chapter to Titus; for there he says, " The grace of God that bring-" eth salvation, appears to all men, and also " teacheth them to deny ungodliness, the world's " lusts," &c. a doctrine which by no means comports with thine in page 5, which speaks of greater opportunities to know, and better qualifications to judge in things which the Scripture says the way-faring man, though a fool, cannot err in. I agree with thee that the information of the wisest is not infallible, when they attain their wisdom in the things of God only from beneath, at schools and colleges, by human arts, learning, &c. But when any possess that wisdom that is from above, and are actuated by it, **such act and speak** with infallible certainty.

If

If the Doctors in Divinity. fo called, know no more of the means of our falvation than thou haft defcribed of it in page 5 and 18, I think it is a pity that there are any; for the people, I believe, would then be more dependent on Him that is able and willing to fave, even to the very uttermoft, of free mercy, without fee or tythes: for in oppofition to thy affertion I teftify, that falvation is the gift of God, and on our parts it requires information that is direct, conviction that is immediate, and the firft degree of knowledge; that it can never grow out of fecond-hand information, nor is weak conviction its proper foil, nor can the heart of a believer be pure, but by virtue of that falvation which well-difpofeth it to bring forth the fruits of that falvation which we have by Chrift Jefus, in the accomplifhment of the angel's declaration, when he told his father that he fhould fave his people from their fins, Matthew i. 21. So that our falvation is of the Lord, and not by a fecond-hand information. I have often thought, and am more and more confirmed in my judgment, that the reafon why there is fo little religion in the world is, becaufe there is fo much preaching in it by men of corrupt minds, and as touching the faith reprobates. I have fometimes admired that the fate of fome of thefe is not the fame as was the fons of Sceva, as their conduct has fome correfpondency. Pleafe to read from the 13th to the 21ft verfe of the xixth chapter of Acts.

I am

I am glad thou fubfcribeft to fallibility, for thy fermon evinceth it to be the cafe. I am fure I feel nothing but love and good-will to thee in my heart, though I thus write; for thy immortal foul is of great value, and therefore I would have thee feek in the humility and fimplicity of a little child to him whom God hath given for a light to enlighten the Gentiles, and for falvation to the ends of the earth; that thou mayeft know him to be fo to thee: for there is no other name, that is power, under heaven, whereby thou canft be faved.

I fhould be glad to ftop here; but my heart feems full of love, both to thee and all mankind; therefore thou muft excufe my proceeding a little farther in the matter before me, as it is of eternal confequence to thee and all men, experimentally to know that Chrift is the way, the truth, and the life; and that no man cometh to the father, but by him: and that in matters of the laft importance to their falvation they muft neither depend on the abilities nor integrity of others; for the call of God is, " Look unto me, " all ye ends of the earth, and be faved," Ifaiah xlv. 22. Paul's learning did not make him a minifter of the gofpel, but a perfecutor of it, and its adherents; but when by the revelation of the Spirit of God. he was ordained a minifter of it, he told the Corinthians to try themfelves, and prove themfelves. as they would by that means know for themfelves that Jefus Chrift was in

them,

them, except they were reprobates : that was by his light and fpirit to teach and inftruct them and us, as he farther wrote, that what was to be known of God was manifeft in man, for that a manifeftation of the fpirit was given to every man to profit withal, 1 Cor. xii. 7, 11—13 ; and this is what he as a true and real doctor in divinity, not a furreptitious one, recommended his patients to ; well knowing that nothing fhort of it could do their fouls effential good ; therefore he would not take their money nor tythes, Acts xx. 33 ; but directed them to Him that hath all power to fave, and freely difpenfeth his faving help to all that will lay hold of it ; and they experience faving health in and by it, nor is falvation in any other.

I did not read thy fermon with any view of remarking on it, after this manner ; but having feen James Hinton's reply to it, I thought it unjuft to give any judgment for or againft either, till I had feen both ; but as I read thy pages, I admired at the openings that arofe in my mind, pointing out the fallacies they contain. In page 6 thou transferreft the antichriftian principles and practices from thyfelf and brethren to other focieties of people, and dubbeft them with the epithet of agents and evil fpirits, under different forms and impofitions ; but I truft I have clearly proved above that thy doctrine bears no fimilitude to the doctrine the apoftle advanceth in the chapter of which thy text is a part.

part. I would have thee read the whole chapter with deep attention, and reverently ponder the fix firſt verſes; for I can in truth ſay my ſpirit very fervently deſireth that divine illumination may quicken thee to ſee how much thou erreſt, both in principle and doctrine, from the ſpirit of that chapter; and indeed I may ſay from the whole tenor of Scripture. I cannot ſay that the ſchools of the prophets that we read of in the Old Teſtament were eſtabliſhed for the education of men to officiate in the prieſt's office at Jerobo-am's idolatrous worſhip; but I believe they were, as we read 1 Kings xii. 31, that he made an houſe of high places, which correſponds very much with the colleges built by the Papiſts under the goſpel diſpenſation; and he made prieſts which were not of the ſons of Levi, and ſo did they of men that were not of the Lord's choice: ſo that the firſt and laſt degeneracy aſſimilate exactly one with the other, and both oppoſed the divine order; as there was no occaſion for ſuch places to inſtruct the Lord's prieſts, he having given full direction himſelf how he would have the ſervice of the tabernacle and temple conducted: but when ſtate policy required that the prieſts ſhould have ſome ſhare in the government, it became neceſſary to have ſuch places eſtabliſhed for their inſtruction into the nature and ſecrets of ſtate policy; as thoſe which were the Lord's faithful prieſts could not deviate from his ſtatutes to obtain any church preferments; and as it was neceſſary that Jero-

boam

boam fhould have fome in whofe eyes a good living and the king's favour was of more value than the falvation of the people, thefe feminaries were devifed for their tuition, that they may the more effectually deceive the people, with a fpecious fhew of temporal confequence, into that idolatry which became to the people of Ifrael a fin; which was productive of the greateft evils and moft afflicting fuffering that they ever experienced : it brought upon them fword, peftilence, famine, and captivity, again and again; as their foolifh hearts were fo wedded to the pompous fhew of thefe idolatrous priefts, when dreffed in their mitres, croziers, cowls, tippets, hoods, caffocks, gowns, furplices, bands, &c. that they departed from the Lord : and that which drew their hearts away from the true worfhip of God, the fame draws away the hearts of carnal people from the worfhipping of God in fpirit and truth unto the prefent day. It was neceffary that Jeroboam fhould have fome fuch as thefe, as the Lord's faithful priefts could not conform to his idolatrous worfhip : we do not read that there were any fchools eftablifhed by divine appointment for the education of either priefts or minifters, under the legal or gofpel difpenfation; therefore it may with ftrict propriety be concluded, that the univerfities in the prefent time had their original rife from the fchools where the priefts and prophets that fed at Jezebel's table had their education.

In

In pages 6 and 7 thou fpeakeft of fome who by the introduction of lies and herefies have corrupted the chriftian faith; but how much of that thou haft practifed in thy fermon before me I fhall leave with others to determine, who have known what the way and work of real falvation is. I much approve of thy diflike of the doctrines and inventions of men being impofed on the people as gofpel and Chriftian; for indeed they are but real antichrifts, and I would therefore afk thee who invented the Common-Prayer-Book, as that is an invention contrary to the apoftle's direction, which was to pray with the fpirit and with the underftanding alfo; but he gave no direction to pray with the book, which falfe priefts, and falfe chriftians can do, but true minifters and true chriftians ftand in no need of it, becaufe they are inftructed what is the mind of the fpirit, which maketh interceffion for them according to the will of God, Rom. viii. 26, 27, and not the will of man; for the will of man, no more than the wrath of man, worketh the righteoufnefs of God; " For it is not of him that " willeth, nor of him that runneth; but it is " God that worketh in us both to will and to do " of his own good pleafure." It is true that faith cometh by hearing, and alfo as true that real, profitable, and eternally efficacious hearing, cometh by the word of God; and therefore the eleventh commandment, if we join it to the ten given to Mofes, or the firft commandment in the New Teftament, was, " This is my be-
" loved

" loved Son in whom I am well pleafed; hear ye
" him;" Matthew xvii. 5: and this is the
word of eternal life, if the apoftles and primitive minifters knew what the word of faving
faith and eternal life was, as thou mayeft fee in
Rom. x. 8: " But what faith it, the word is nigh
" thee, even in thy mouth and in thy heart—
" that is the word of faith which we preach:"
&c. and in Gal. i. 8, he fays, " If any man
" preach any other gofpel than that we have
" preached. let him be accurfed:" and in
fpeaking of what the gofpel was, declared it to
be the power of God unto falvation; and this
muft be Chrift, as all power both in heaven and
in earth is given unto him, nor is there falvation in any other; and from whofe convicting
power in the heart none can flee, no more than
Adam after his tranfgreffion could flee from the
Divine prefence and hide himfelf from his
judgments.

If they whofe words thou haft perverted to
make a trade of, had any knowledge from
whence falvation was. and from whom received,
as thou mayeft fee, John vi. 68, where they faid,
" Lord, whither fhall we go, for thou haft the
" words of eternal life;" and David faid, ad-
dreffing himfelf to the Moft High, " Thy word
" have I hid in my heart, that I may not fin
" againft thee," Pfalm cxix. 11. and by bearing
and regarding that word which brought him
faith, not of mens making, but God's gift, he
had

had this evidence; and therefore declared of it, that others may wifely imitate his example, Pfalm cxix. 99—104. " I have more underftand-" ing than all my teachers, for thy teftimonies " are my meditations." The word which God commanded all men to hear, was the word which took flefh and dwelt amongft men for a feafon; which word is gone forth into all the world, even to the ends of the earth; nor is there fpeech or language where it is not heard, nor is there any other word that can infpire our minds with divine faith, in Him in whom alone falvation is, and not in any other; fo that the abilities and integrity of the teachers of whom thou fpeakeft are totally infufficient for this thing, though they may be deep proficients in Ariftotle's logic, and that philofophy and vain deceit which is after the rudiments of the world, the traditions of men, and not after Chrift, Colof. ii. 8.

I fhall begin my remarks on thy 8th page, with that pertinent query, Job. xi. 7. " Canft " thou by fearching find out God? Canft thou " find out the Almighty to perfection?" I conclude thy modefty will anfwer, No. Then I would fay, How canft thou pretend to teach Him, and his will, whom thou canft not find out? Muft not this be prefumption of a moft flagrant degree, and deception of an abominable magnitude! Excufe my freedom, for it feems to me that thy foul is at ftake; and my defire is to awaken it to a holy dependence on the arm of

Divine

Divine fufficiency; for our fufficiency is not of ourfelves but of Him, 2 Corinth. iii. 5, 6. The prophet, under the legal difpenfation, called on the people " to ceafe from man, whofe breath " is in his noftrils; for," faid he, " wherein is he " to be accounted of:" and more than that, for, " Curfed," faid he, " is man that trufteth in " man, and maketh flefh his arm, and whofe " heart is departed from the Lord; he fhall be " like the heath in the defert, that knoweth not " when good cometh," Jeremiah xvii. 5, 6, 7, 8.

I have no pleafure in writing this, fave that which arifeth from a confcioufnefs of doing that which I believe is the divine will in it; as the openings are fuch in my mind while I am writing, that I am perfuaded it is from him; for the cloathing with which my mind is covered is that love which defires the falvation of all men as my own. In page 9, thou fpeakeft of univerfities as being places of learning, for the regular qualification and due authority for the miniftry, and for fupplying the body of the clergy, according to forms, and offices that are purely fcriptural; in which I conceive thou haft exceeded the bounds of truth; for in the fcriptures I cannot find any one thing that countenances the practices of the univerfities, from the firft admiffion of a ftudent, to the inducting him into a parochial, or fome other living; except thou allow them and Jeroboam's fchools to be on the fame foundation; but I find many things in the
fcriptures

scriptures which fully contradict the practices of
the univerfities: but as they were built at a time
when ignorance was the mother of devotion, and
the laity were not allowed to read the fcriptures,
it is no wonder that practices fo contrary to
them were fallen in with, as the corrupt clergy
of that time inftructed the people to believe that
by fuch acts they may purchafe abfolution for
their own fouls and their friends. O horrid
delufion! which makes me admire that men profeffing to be more enlightened, ftill fupport fa-
bricks which were built on fuch a corrupt foundation; or that people will fuffer themfelves to
be fo beguiled, as to think that human learning
and human ordination can make a man a minifter
of the gofpel of Chrift, when the facred declaration of the Apoftles is, " That no man taketh
" this honour upon himfelf, but he that is called
" of God as was Aaron," Hebrews v. 4 : fo that
it is not univerfity education, or ordination,
that makes men minifters of the gofpel, but the
call and ordination of God only; and Paul,
from his own experience, declares that he received not his miniftry of man, neither was he
taught it, but by the Revelation of Jefus Chrift;
nor did he go to the apoftles for ordination,
but went into Arabia, and from thence returned
to Damafcus, fo that he was an itinerant preacher,
with a witnefs; yet no whit behind the chiefeft
of the apoftles: but it is no wonder that men
that do not receive their miniftry in the way he
did his, have not unity with his practices; for
light

light and darknefs, letter and fpirit, have no
fellowfhip; as one killeth, the other giveth life.
Paul could not preach Chrift, till he had him
firft revealed in him; for the learning he had
acquired in the fchool of Gamaliel, was no qualification for gofpel miniftry, though it was fuffi-
cient to make him very mad againft the itinerant preachers of that time: but when he became one himfelf, and had no rectorial prefer-
ment, he could then declare he was not fo. " I
" am not mad, moft noble Feftus, but fpeak
" forth the words of truth and fobernefs:" and
when he was brought to this ftate he accounted
his learning but as drofs and dung compared to
the excellency of the knowledge he had received in the Revelation of Chrift Jefus his
Lord; for by it he was inftructed that without
it he could do nothing; but through it ftrengthen-
ing him, he could do all things. Philippians,
iv. 13.

Page 10 thou telleft thy audience, of neceffity
they muft be taught by fome; but how flatly
this contradicts God himfelf in that holy book
which thou profeffeft thy rule to walk by, Ifaiah
liv. 13, " And all thy children fhall be taught
" by the Lord, and great fhall be the peace of
" thy children:" and John vi. 45, " It is written
" in the Prophets, and they fhall all be taught of
" God; every man, therefore that hath learned
" of the Father, cometh unto me." Ifaiah xlviii.
17, " Thus faith the Lord thy Redeemer, the
" Holy

" Holy One of Ifrael, I am the Lord thy God
" that teacheth thee to profit, which leadeth
" thee by the way that thou fhouldeft go."
Verfe 18, " Oh that thou hadft harkened to my
" counfel, then had thy peace been as a river,
" and thy rightcoufnefs as the waves of the fea."
Now the reafon why they did not hearken unto
his counfel was, becaufe the priefts were corrupt, and corrupted the people; for this fame
prophet complains in the Lord's name as follows, " Oh my people, they that lead thee
" caufe thee to err, and deftroy the way of thy
" paths." And the Lord feeing the wickednefs
and degeneracy of the priefts, gracioufly promifed to teach the people himfelf, and not leave
them to the inftruction of men of corrupt minds,
and as touching the faith, reprobates, that
preach for hire, and divine for money, and
teach for doctrine the traditions of men,
things which they ought not for filthy lucre's
fake. Micah iii. 11, 12, " The priefts there-
" of teach for hire, the prophets thereof divine
" for money, yet will they lean upon the Lord,
" and fay, Is not the Lord amongft us? no evil
" can come upon us:" verfe 12, " Therefore fhall
" Zion for your fakes be ploughed as a field, and
" Jerufalem fhall become heaps, and the moun-
" tain of the houfe, as the high places of the fo-
" reft." Now the prieft's fin here complained
of was teaching for hire, and the prophets that
of divining for money; but men of this fort

C

muft

muſt preach to pleaſe the people, or elſe they
will not pay them for it, where they are not by
popiſh laws compell'd to it; but how contrary is
this to the practice of the true miniſters of the
goſpel, " Do I then," ſaid Paul, " ſeek to pleaſe
" men or God; if I yet ſeek to pleaſe men,
" then ſhould I not be the ſervant of Chriſt."
And in John xiv. 26, we read, " But the Com-
" forter, which is the Holy Ghoſt, whom my Fa-
" ther will ſend in my name, he will teach you all
" things, and bring all things to your remem-
" brance, whatſoever I have ſaid unto you."
And this is confirmed by the beloved diſciple,
in the epiſtle of which the text is a part, chapter
ii. verſe 20. " But ye have an unction from
" the Holy One, and ye know all things." But I
muſt refer thee to the two proceeding verſes
for a portrait of thyſelf; they run thus, " Lit-
" tle children, it is the laſt time, and as ye have
" heard that Antichriſt ſhall come, even now
" there are many Antichriſts, whereby we know
" that it is the laſt time; they went out from us,.
" but they were not of us; for if they had been
" of us, they would no doubt have continued
" with us; but they went out, that they may be
" made manifeſt that they were not of us:" as
Jeroboam and his ſcholars, though they were
Jews, manifeſted themſelves not to be true wor-
ſhippers of God, but went out from them into
idolatry for the ſake of lucre. Now I draw this
character or complexion of antichriſt from the
diſagreement of his doctrine and thine; his was
that

that Chriſtians had an unſtion from the Holy
One, by which they knew all things neceſſary
for their ſalvation, in this world: thy doſtrine
is, that Chriſtians muſt be taught the things concerning their ſalvation by learned men; but that
ſaying of our Lord's comes ſtrong into my
mind, " Ye fools and blind, whether is greater
" the temple, or the altar that ſanſtifieth the
" temple?" He that readeth, let him alſo under-
ſtand; it was learned men that did not know our
bleſſed Saviour, but wrote an inſcription in He-
brew, Greek, and Latin deridingly, acknow-
ledging him to be king of the Jews, but could
not by their learning ſee him to be what he
was, The Lord of Life and Glory. And the
ſame wiſe, learned, and carnal ſpirit is writing over him now in the ſame language, their
ſufficiency as ſuperior to every other thing
to give the knowledge of him, in this day: but
this eternal truth will ſtand over it for ever, that
" No man knoweth the Father, but the Son, and
" he to whom the Son will reveal him." And
by this the poor illiterate fiſhermen were better
acquainted with the myſteries of the kingdom of
God, than the wiſe and learned Rabbies amongſt
the Jews. Nor did the learned Saul, the Uphol-
ſterer or Tent-maker, know them, till he counted
his learning droſs and dung in compariſon of it.
" Art thou," ſaid our Lord to Nicodemus, " a
" maſter of Iſrael, and knoweſt not theſe things?"
and now I would ſay to EDWARD, a teacher in
Oxford, Art thou a maſter in Oxford, and

knoweſt

knoweſt not theſe things? Thy Sermon declares
this to be the caſe: and now I may tell thee that
my very heart fervently prays for thee, as the
prophet did for his ſervant, 2 Kings vi. 17. " Lord
" I pray thee open his eyes." Thou wiſhedſt
that the people of Oxford would do themſelves
the juſtice of trying you by the ſame rule that
mechanicks abilities are tried; but if they did,
I think they would be as blind as thoſe blind
leaders of the blind, which our Lord ſaid ſhould
both fall into the ditch; for their imaginations
muſt be very dark, which cannot ſee the different
ſource from which ſpiritual and natural knowledge is derived, the one by ſtudy, practice, and
labour in the ſeveral arts that they would ac-
quire; but the other is the immediate gift of
God; and whoever is unacquainted with this
truth, the ſame cannot poſſibly be a ſteward of
the myſteries of God, however they may delude
themſelves with the idea, as Saul did; but when
it pleaſed God who ſeparated him from his mother's womb, to call him by his grace, to reveal
his Son in him, that he ſhould preach him
amongſt the Gentiles, he forthwith conferred
not with fleſh and blood; neither went he to
Oxford, Cambridge, Edinburgh, or Aberdeen,
for ordination; his authority and qualification
being higher than any fallen creature could
confer upon him; nor can the myſtery of God,
or true qualification for the miniſtry of his
goſpel, be attained by all the ſtudy, or learning,
in the world, for it is only as he is pleaſed to
open

open and reveal them in the fouls of thofe that
he makes, by the baptizing virtue of his own immediate power, fit veffels to be put into the
miniftry, 1 Tim. i. 12. " And I thank Chrift
" Jefus our Lord, who hath enabled me, for that
" he counted me faithful, putting me into the
" miniftry."

This is a doctrine that the wifdom of this
world hath antiquated, and fo oppofeth it; but
if immediate Revelation is ceafed, falvation is
alfo ceafed, for Chrift himfelf hath declared,
" That no man knoweth the Father but the Son,
" and he to whom the Son will reveal him;"
and that eternal life confifts in our knowing of
God, and Jefus Chrift whom he hath fent.
When parting with the apoftles he told them
to go and teach all nations, baptizing them in
the name of the Father, Son, and Holy Ghoft,
for that he would be with them alway, even to
the end of the world; and this was neceffary, as
without his power and prefence they could not
do it; for he had told them before that without him they could do nothing; that is, with re-
gard to his glory, or increafe of his fpiritual
kingdom, becaufe the things of it are as the nature of it is, pure and eternal. Elementary
things are in the power of men to ufe and to
difufe as they pleafe, but " the things of God
" knoweth no man, fave the fpirit of God,"
1 Cor. ii. 11. " and they to whom he is pleafed
" to reveal them." Now minifters of mens mak-

C 3

ing

ing can fprinkle or dip in water, but this is
not Holy Ghoft and fire baptifm, nor is it in
the power of any mere man to effect it, which
our Lord well knew, and therefore promifed his
miniffers his gracious and omnipotent prefence,
to aid them in this work ; nor can any be his
minifters or ftewards of the myfteries of God,
but thofe he thus aids, and qualifies, and they
may be learned or unlearned, as in his wifdom
he may fee meet to call and ordain; and others,
to fay the fofteft word I can for them, are but
vain deceiving intruders ; therefore I muft fay
it is with amazement and concern that I fee
one, that profeffeth himfelf a fteward of the
myfteries of God, fo profoundly ignorant of
them, as to fuppofe and teach that human learning can furnifh a man with the knowledge of
them.

I am no Sectarian, but believe that in every
nation, kindred, tongue, and people, they that
fear God, and work righteoufnefs, are accepted
of him ; but as thou haft denominated itinerant
preachers of every denomination ignorant ; Me-
thodifts, Enthufiafts, Anabaptifts, and Diffenters,
as perfons whom the inhabitants of Oxford have
not the fmalleft proof of, I would put thee in
mind that fome itinerant preachers in former
times, that were not very learned, had knowledge taken of them, that they had been with
Jefus. Acts, iv. 13. " When they faw the
" boldnefs of Peter and John, and perceived
" that

" that they were unlearned and ignorant men,
" they marvelled and took knowledge of them,
" that they had been with Jesus." Now these
were not univerfity or learning made minifters;
fo the learned minifters of that time, that knew
not the power of God, oppofed them, as thou
doft in this; but their anfwer was, " Whether
" it be right in the fight of God to hearken
" unto you, more than unto God, judge ye."

I hope thou wilt now acknowledge I have
fairly tried thy fpirit by the Scriptures, and that
I have found it very oppofite to them; therefore
it muft be the very antichrift againft which John
cautioned all true Chriftians to the world's end:
nor can fuch that are fo, fubfcribe to thy fpiritual abilities, for thy doctrines carry fo much
carnality in them, that to me they feem to minifter death, as Paul faith the carnal mind doth.
I believe that no wife or good man fets learning
at defiance, or holds fcience in contempt; for
my own part, I wifh I had more of it, as I never
learnt my native tongue grammatically, therefore I hold neither learning nor fcience in
contempt, as learning and fcience, but believe them ufeful both for pleafure and profit; but when they are made the ground of qualification for gofpel miniftry, then I believe in
that point of view all wife and good men hold
them in contempt, as Saul did, who was pof-
feffed of a large fhare of them, as thou mayeft
fee in Philippians iii. 8. Thy fallacy, or ignorance, or both, is moft obvious in that thou de-

3   clareft

clareft thy belief is that the fcriptures are the
true light that lighteth every man that cometh
into the world; when the fcriptures themfelves
declare the direct contrary, and fay that the
Word that took flefh and dwelt amongft men,
which was Chrift, was the true light, that lighteth
every man that cometh into the world; as may
be feen in John's declaration of the gofpel,
chap. i. 9. What perverfion of fcripture is this!
John told the primitive Chriftians they knew all
things, through the teaching of the Divine
Unction, which they had received by Chrift, the
true light; 1 Epift. John ii. 26, 27, " *Thefe*
" *things have I written unto you concerning them*
" *that feduce you. But the anointing which ye*
" *have received of him abideth in you, and ye need*
" *not that any man teach you: but, as the fame*
" *anointing teacheth you of all things, and is truth,*
" *and is no lye: and even as it hath taught you, ye fhall*
" *abide in him:*" but thou feemeft, notwithftand-
ing thy learning, to be in the ftate that Caiaphas
told his and thy brethren they were in, when in
the council they had called to confult what they
fhould do againft Chrift and his itinerant
minifters, they being the ruling and beneficed
clergy of that time: what he told them was,
that they knew nothing at all; and that feems to
be the cafe with thee, that thy ignorance fhould
exalt the fcriptures into the place of Chrift!
If this is not antichrift and falfe doctrine, I know
not what is; for although there is a fpirit in man,
it is the infpiration of the Almighty that giveth

it

it an underftanding, as thou mayeft read in Job xxxii. 8; and if it was not for this infpiration, how could the fcriptures poffibly be underftood, or the people be qualified to judge of fpiritual things; for they are only fpiritually difcerned by the illuminating virtue of this infpiring power of the Sun of Righteoufnefs, which arifeth with healing in his wings to thofe that fear his name, Malachi iv. 2. Indeed the carnal preacher may make reprefentations of them, but cannot give the people the living experience of it, no more than a limner can give the dead reprefentation of a man or woman animal life. May I not therefore with great propriety apply that fcripture to thee, Mark xii. 24. "And Jefus anfwering faid "unto them, Do ye not therefore err, becaufe "ye know not the fcriptures, neither the power "of God?" This may feem plain dealing, but truth calls for it, and the nature of the cafe requires it, therefore count me not an enemy but a friend, becaufe I tell thee the truth.

In page 12 thou warneft the people to beware of falfe prophets; but of what clafs thou art, I will leave the witnefs for God in thy own heart to judge, for judgment is not mine but his; yet he hath given us a criterion by which we may judge fome things; "For by their fruits," faid he, "ye fhall know them:" and I am perfuaded the fpiritual eye can as clearly as the natural one difcern that men do not gather grapes of thorns nor figs of thiftles. The fcriptures thou haft
quoted

quoted are well chofen, but mifapplied, page 12; for they revert back, if the above concluſions are true, and apply ſtrictly to him that I am writing to; therefore I intreat of thee to adopt that part of thy church ſervice in ſincerity of heart, and addreſs it to him who hath all men's in his power, that he may cleanſe thine by the inſpiration of his holy ſpirit; for there is no other way that it can poſſibly be done. I conclude with thee that to judge of the ſecret ſpring and principles of the heart, and of thoſe motives that lay buried within the breaſt, is indeed a difficult and delicate taſk; and that falſe teachers are to be tried by the rule that Chriſt hath given us, I alſo ſubſcribe to, and for that reaſon have followed his rule in trying thee, believing that rule a ſolemn duty of religion, and that the fruits of the ſpirits of men and women that are real members of his church are love, joy, peace, long-ſuffering, gentleneſs, goodneſs, faith, meekneſs, temperance. Now I would have thee aſk thyſelf which of theſe fruits ſtimulated thee to compoſe thy ſermon ſuitable to the times; but I think a very unſuitable thing to appear in the chriſtian world; for if I have a right favour, it doth not ſeem to reliſh of any one of them, but its compoſition ſeems to derive its original from juſt the oppoſite, viz. hatred, variance, emulation, wrath, ſtrife, ſedition, hereſies, &c. I think it ſomewhat poſſeſſeth the ſpirit of Paſhur, the ſon of Immur the prieſt, when he ſmote Jeremiah, and put him in the ſtocks; in
which

which act I can perceive no love, and therefore not a fruit of the Divine Spirit, though it was said of him that he was a governor in the house of the Lord; and some say thou art so too. Pure and disinterested love flows in my soul to thee at this very instant, which gives me to hope that my labour here will not be altogether in vain, in the Lord. I wish not to meddle with politics in state affairs; but am of the judgment that the calumnies and odiums thou hast thrown on the Dissenters and others, are neither just nor true, for I believe that though there may be some disaffected persons in all dissenting societies, yet I believe their numbers are but very small compared with the whole; and their designs by no means what thou representest. For my own part, I can say I have no wish for any other form of government but monarchical; nor have I any acquaintance that do; or why we should, I do not see; as the British throne hath now for more than a century been filled with mild and gentle kings, though I know that it is the mind of many, that a reform in the government would be a great benefit to the state. Thou, and I suppose most people in the nation, do know that many of the established clergy, and people, are avowedly inimical to the present government; but I hope divine mercy will preserve us from anarchy, confusion, and disorder. But before I drop this, I may say, that one great reason why the people are not so well satisfied with the government is, because they conti-
nue

nue that grievous, oppreſſive, and antichriſtian burthen of tythes to ſupport men, that they are perſuaded are not by any divine law heirs to any ſuch inheritance; and now I may ſimply ſay what my faith is, that the Lord will ſweep away both them and their receivers together. And here I drop that head.

I cannot ſubſcribe to the church of England being the apoſtolic and holy catholic church, yet I believe that many of her members are members of the church which is ſo, according to the light and knowledge that they have received; by which they have come beyond her forms and ceremonies, to be partakers of that inward and ſpiritual grace of which all muſt be partakers: as it is that alone by which all that enter into her communion know their initiation, and its power as far to excel the outward and viſible ſign, as light doth darkneſs. And I believe there are in all church communions, perſons of this claſs; and that ſuch perſons make up the truly catholic and apoſtolic church all the world over, that are led by the Spirit of God into all their religious exercifes, and no other: for he told Peter that his church ſhould be built upon that rock, ·which was the revelation of his Father's Spirit, and that the gates of hell ſhould not prevail againſt it: nor is it poſſible they ſhould, as he hath promiſed to be with it even to the end of the world. Now thou knoweſt what my faith is about the church, its foundation, and its members.

As

As to the spirits thou speakest of, that are abroad in the world, that would deprive us of our happiness; I am unacquainted with any such, therefore shall let them alone: but the scriptures thou hast referred us to, to try them by, revert back upon thyself; thy doctrine being exactly that which constitutes thee to be the man that is not of God; for the man that is of God says, that Jesus Christ is come in the flesh, and he is that anointing or unction in man that taught and doth teach all that will learn of him, what the will of God, and their duty towards him is: but thou sayest it is the scriptures that enlighten every man coming into the world: but I would ask thee how the Gentiles were enlighted by them, that never had them? and yet they testify that the Gentiles that never had them, nor any other outward law, were a law unto themselves; which shewed the works of the law written in their hearts, their conscience also bearing them witness, &c. Rom. ii. 14, 15. The prophet Isaiah, under the Old Testament dispensation, had a more perfect knowledge of Christ, his work and office, than thou seemest to have under the New, although a professed master in Israel; for he declared in prophecy that God the Father would send Christ the anointed to be a leader and a commander of the people: and in chap. xlii. 6, 7. speaking of him and what he was to effect in and for them that believe in, and receive him, and not the scriptures only, though they are a true and

faithful

faithful revelation and declaration of him, " I
" the Lord have called thee in righteoufnefs, I
" will hold thy hand, and will keep thee, and
" give thee for a covenant of the people, for a
" light of the Gentiles, to open the blind eyes,
" to bring out the prifoners from the prifon, and
" them that fit in darknefs out of the prifon-
" houfe." Chap. xlix. 6, 7. " And he faid, it is
" a light thing that thou fhouldft be my fervant,
" to raife up the tribes of Jacob, I will give thee
" for a light of the Gentiles, that thou mayeft
" be my falvation unto the ends of the earth;
" thus faith the Lord of Hofts, the Redeemer of
" Ifrael, and his Holy One, to him whom man
" defpifeth, to him whom the nations abhorreth,
" to a fervant of rulers, kings fhall fee and
" arife, princes fhall alfo worfhip, becaufe of
" the Lord which is faithful, and the Holy One
" of Ifrael, and he fhall choofe thee."

I might quote moft part of the fcriptures that
fpeaks of him, to fhew the fallacy and abfurdity
of thy doctrine; but I wifh to have done : but
thou appeareft to me to be the perfon that would
deprive us of our happinefs in this world, by
blowing the fire of contention and animofity
amongft the people; and I believe in my heart, if
we were to follow the divinity doctrine advanced
in thy Sermon, we fhould be bereaved of our
falvation in the next, as the fcriptures declare,
Philip. ii. 9, 10, 11. " Wherefore God hath
" highly exalted him, and given him a name
" which

3

" which is above every name, that at the name
" of Jefus every knee fhall bow, of things in
" heaven, and things on earth, and things under
" the earth; and that every tongue fhall confefs
" that Jefus Chrift is Lord, to the glory of God
" the Father." And again, Acts v. 31. " Him
" hath God exalted to be a prince and a Saviour,
" to give repentance to Ifrael, and forgivenefs
" of fins:" but Edward Tatham hath exalted
the fcriptures, and his brethrens commentaries,
&c. on them, into the place of Chrift, in faying
they are the true light that enlighteneth every
man coming into the world; which abundantly
confirmeth me in what I have long believed,
and have fome time fince advanced; and that
is, that all fyftematick preaching is an idol of
human compofition, and that by which the people in too general a way are made to truft in a
lie, as may be feen in Jeremiah xxiii. 14. " I
" have feen alfo in the prophets of Jeru-
" falem an horrible thing, they commit adul-
" tery, and walk in lies; they ftrengthen alfo
" the hands of the evil doers, that none doth
" turn from his wickednefs; they are all of them
" unto me as Sodom, and the inhabitants there-
" of as Gomorrah." Ver. 21. " I have not fent
" thefe prophets, yet they run. I have not
" fpoken unto them, yet they have prophefied."
Ver. 32. " Behold, I am againft them that pro-
" phefy falfe dreams, faith the Lord, and do tell
" them, and caufe my people to err by their
" lies, and by their lightnefs; yet I fent them

not,

" not, nor commanded them, therefore they
" fhall not profit this people at all, faith the
" Lord." Ifaiah iii. and laft part of the 12th
verfe, " Oh! my people, they that lead thee
" caufe thee to err, and deftroy the way of thy
" paths." And again, lvi. 9. 10, 11, 12. " All
" the beafts in the field come to devour, yea
" all the beafts in the forefts; his watchmen are
" blind, they are all ignorant, they are all dumb
" dogs, they cannot bark; lying down, loving to
" flumber; yea, they are greedy dogs, that can
" never have enough, and they are fhepherds
" that cannot underftand; they all look to their
" own way, every one for his gain from his
" quarter. Come ye, fay they, I will fetch
" wine, and we will fill ourfelves with ftrong
" drink, and to-morrow fhall be as this day, and
" much more abundant." I fhall now leave it.
with thee to contraft things of that and the prefent time, as I wifh to avoid comparifons and
reflections, as much as I can, with juftice to the
caufe I am engaged in. But give me leave to
quote two more verfes, Malachi ii. 8, 9. " But
" ye are departed out of the way; ye have
" caufed many to ftumble at the law, ye have
" corrupted the covenant of Levi, faith the
" Lord of Hofts; therefore alfo have I made
" you contemptible and bafe before all the
" people, according as ye have not kept my
" ways, but have been partial in the laws." If
the tenor of thy Sermon had run parallel with
a truth thou advanceft towards the clofe, I believe

lieve I fhould not have made any obfervations on it. The truth I allude to is, thy afferting the divinity of Chrift, and unity with the godhead, as co eternal with the Father before the world was: for truly he was God manifeft in the flefh for man's redemption; being as the prophet fpeaks concerning him, Ifaiah xlii. 11. " I, even " I am the Lord, and befide me there is no " Saviour." chap. xlv. 21. " Who hath declared " this from ancient time? who hath told it from " that time? have not I, the Lord; and there " is no God befide me. Look unto me and be " faved, all the ends of the earth, for I am God " and there is none other."

Knowing that all the help of man is vain, therefore I have long ceafed from man, and all his carnal ordinances, which to me feem to be devifed by the evil one, to fupport his kingdom under a falfe appearance; they being only images of righteoufnefs, but have no degree of the life of righteoufnefs in them; though acted under that mafk and character, by which the hearts of the fimple are the more eafily deceived, and have been practifed by men as things of a divine nature for filthy lucre fake; therefore I came out from among them and was feparated in obedience to the divine command, that I may have no Father in God but him. 2 Corinthians, vi. 17, 18. " Wherefore come out from amongft " them, and be ye feparate, faith the Lord, and " touch not the unclean things, and I will re-
" ceive

" ceive you, and I will be a father únto you,
" and ye fhall be my fons and daughters, faith
" the Lord Almighty."

Thy chain of arguing, in page 17, breathes
but little or no charity; and thou knoweft
what Paul fays to thofe that do not poffefs it,
1 Corinthians. xiii. 1. " Though I fpeak with
" the tongue of men or angels, and have not
" charity, I am become as founding brafs or a
" tinkling cymbal " But I charitably hope and
truft there are but few, if any, men profeffing
Chriftianity, that can fubfcribe to fuch a creed
as thou haft compiled for them; yet I muft with
forrow acknowledge there is too much Deifm in
the world: and do believe it hath had its birth,
from time to time, from fuch Sermons as one that
was read in Oxford in the year 1792, under the
title of " A Sermon fuitable to the Times." I
would have all men fear God, and honour the
King as his minifter; but I do not believe that
this will fecure our happinefs, either in this
world or in the world to come: for by this means
the rankeft Deift upon earth may attain to
heaven. if fearing God and honouring the king,
would fecure it for him.

In page 18 thou addreffeft thy audience as follows : " The conduct, my brethren, which will
" fecure your happinefs, both in this world and
" the next, is prefcribed in one fhort command
" of Holy Scripture, Fear God and honour the
" king." Could the rankeft Deift upon earth
preach

preach a doctrine more oppofite to the doctrines of Chriftianity, than this of thine is?
And if thy heart believes what thy mouth hath
uttered, thou muft be one of thofe very men
thy creed in page 17 fuits. I am forry that
darknefs hath fo veiled thy mind; but it is a
common proverb, That there is nothing blinder
than prejudice. I would have thee write no
more, or elfe with more congruity and a Chriftian fpirit, and not upon the broad fcale of cen-
furing and condemning all focieties of people
but thy own; nor as a fawning fycophant purfue
court favours, Amaziah like, Amos vii. 10, 11,
12, 13, " Then Amaziah, the prieft of Bethel,"
(fhall I fay, EDWARD TATHAM, prieft of Oxford) " fent to Jeroboam, king of Ifrael, fay-
" ing, Amos hath confpired againft thee in the
" midft of the houfe of Ifrael: the land is not
" able to bear all his words, for thus Amos
" faith, that Jeroboam fhall die by the fword,
" and all Ifrael fhall furely be led away captive
" out of their own land. Alfo Amaziah faid
" unto Amos, O, thou Seer, go, flee away
" into the land of Judah, and there eat bread,
" and prophefy there, but prophefy not any
" more at Bethel, for it is the king's chapel,
" and it is the king's court." Under the law, if
a thief had ftolen any thing, and had not where-
with of his own to make reftitution to the owner
for that which he had ftolen, he was to be fold,
and fo reftitution was to be made out of the money that was took for him : now what reftitution

canft

canſt thou make for the injuries thou haſt done by inſinuation and direct charges, in thy ſermon, againſt Methodiſt, Enthuſiaſt, Anabaptiſt, and Diſſenter, indiſcriminately? For ſurely thou haſt by falſe declarations in thy Sermon robbed thouſands of people that are claſſed under the above denominations of their good names and loyalty, that I believe are more ſo than their denouncer, if a fair inveſtigation of the matter was to take place.

But let me conclude with ſaying, I believe what thou ſayeſt the apoſtle tells us, is a truth, which is, that falſe teachers are deceivers; and I am perſuaded if EDWARD TATHAM candidly and impartially peruſes this, he will clearly perceive who is one.

F I N I S.